ANGEL FLESH

POEMS 1978–1998

PADMA JARED THORNLYRE

ARTWORK

Cover art and illustrations by Reven Swanson. Cover design by Padma J. Thornlyre. Back cover author photograph by Eric Walter, digitally altered by Padma J. Thornlyre.

HOW KOLA!

...to Julie (who married me), Circe and Annésta; to Artemis, Pan, Aphrodite and Hekate; to The Ancient Order of Fire Gigglers; to Menton, Montaña, and my "brother" JM in California; to Lilia and Tássaná for the Italian; to China Cat Sunflower; and to the gentlefolk at Eco Graphics...*IN NOMINE DEÆ BEATÆ, MATRIS OMNIUM.*

CREDITS

The following publications—print and electronic—have presented work from *Angel Flesh*: *Amore*[3], *Black Cross*, *Blue Light Review*, *Coe Review*, *Concurrence Magazine*, *Diogenesis*, *Expresso Tilt*, *Famous Last Words*, *Golden Isis*, *Green Cart Magazine*, *Mad Blood*, *Malcontent*, *Midnight Zoo*, *Mountain Muse*, *National Library of Poetry*, *Pegasus*, *Recursive Angel*, *Sauce Box*, *Tabula Rasa*, *Thirteen*, *Wisconsin Review*, *Yellow Silk*, and *Yoni*.

Baculite Publishing Company
10853 West Dorado Avenue
Columbine Hills Sta., Colorado 80127

TABLE OF CONTENTS

PART 1: TWO EAST

(ILLUSTRATIONS: VIII, 12, 21)

PART 2: ORGASM HALLUCINATIONS

(ILLUSTRATIONS: 28, 50)

PART 3: COLD WOMB. WET WORLD.

(ILLUSTRATIONS: 52, 58, 60, 63, 68)

PART 4: MNEMOSYNE

(ILLUSTRATIONS: 80, 94)

Foreword

Angel Flesh stares down madness. Its poems are ecstatic, grotesque, bloody, and disoriented by blizzards. Were I to expose this book in the desert, I'd expect crow and condor to make short work of it. I recommend adding one page, well-shredded, to a pot of green chile. Expect indigestion. Better yet, ingest with ouzo—one shot per poem. Masticate vigorously.

Angel Flesh was inspired by actual events in my life, but poetry is, as it has always been, witchcraft—shamanism and myth-making; therefore, I remind the reader to take this work, not literally, but metaphorically, and not as an historical or journalistic document, but as an attempt at art. Accordingly, names have been altered to conceal the identities of those whose actions informed its composition. Consider, too, that poems re-create states of mind, inevitably the author's own. Memory is subjective and relative.

Angel Flesh concerns real issues of love and death. A woman I loved attempted suicide: in some poems, she survives; in others she does not. My subsequent horror led me open-eyed and stunned into my *own* madness—through the gates of fragmentation, dissociation, panic disorder, nightmares and sleeplessness...I am fortunate to have lived much of this madness through verse.

If you do not consider love, death, and psychic meltdown proper fodder for poetry or myth, don't bother reading Angel Flesh. Some poems are explicitly violent and/or explicitly sexual, so exercise sound judgment and bury the book as *terma* in your neighbor's back yard.

Padma Jared Thornlyre
Golden, Colorado
December 3, 1997

ANGEL FLESH

FOR ANNÉSTA OF RED SANDSTONE CREEK

HER BREASTS AND HER DARK HAIR
WERE PERFUME...

ARCHILOCHOS, THASOS, 8TH CENTURY B.C.E.

OCEAN OF SNOW: LET IT DRIFT SLOWER AND
DEEPER. PILES BEYOND OUR WHITEST DREAMS.
COZY, COOL, AND ALL-ABSORBING. A WELL
FOR LIGHT AND ALL THAT MOVES.

JAMES KOBIELUS, U.S.A., 20TH CENTURY C.E.

Part 1:

Two East

Untouched by the death

of our unholy needs,

we are, indeed, pagans.

(S, Iowa, 20th Century C.E.)

GARDEN

A rock breathes.
A pond
Remains glassy.
No wind
Can touch the rock.
No dream the pond.

CANVAS

a secret she

cleanses this urn

of its poisons.

SNOW MEADOW

white rose
swells
into lotus

Two East

They call you "Crazy Kassandra"
and "paranoid schizophrenic";

you call yourself "the Virgin
Mary, a telepathic whore".

You become what you create,
but you are not on your own side.

"Christlike and chameleon,"
the lazing snows on your

Two East window are
"blizzards, breasts adrift."

I am "too intense" for you
and you are "too intense"

for yourself. I
believed you sane,

                                        wrongly sedated,

                        your hair anointing

                                    my lap

but the
drift

        settled...

                    you want me
                            "nowhere near,

a crow,
an emptied sky."

ODYSSEUS TO SELENA

I am not Endymion
Whose dream of kissing himself
Sired your fifty daughters.

I am not immortal —
Kalypso offered godhead
After maidenhead, but Ithaka

Was necessity — after Nausikaa
The rags and the bloodshed,
The bath and Penelope's bed.

I observed you on rugged Latmos,
Month after month, veiled
In black, take the Artemis-leap

To the grotto of your obsession;
Your thighs Atalantean,
But how could Endymion know?

Crescent-crowned, winged with obsidian
Night, the girls on Lesbos adored you —
At the altar by the moonflower

Trellis, adored the wine you'd
Become to them, adored your cupped
Palms, that shower of moonstones

Over their lavender, sea-misted hair.
But I am Odysseus — my own scalp
Scarred by the surf and stone,

And you are unsatisfied. For I
Have not the grace of a girl, her
Softer tongue, nor Endymion's silence.

I am awkward — undisguised, skyclad,
My lips adoring your cloudlike breasts,
Your head at rest on my coarse chest.

My heart cannot contain you.
Nor would it! My heart contains
Only the hunger which you and I share,

The hunger which bade us seek
In each other a rebuttal
To the slander, *Pan is dead!*

Weary of the cross, that unwieldy god,
Bored of morality, hungry for flesh,
We turned from his golden throne,

And from his pronouncement, *Pan is dead!*
Syrinx-led, we fled to the forest,
To a leafy bed by an eddying pool.

What passed was Pan, his ritual —
You caressed his great horns
As they lay upon your lap,

As I became he and brushed with my lips
The silk of your crescent. Yet you turn
Suddenly, remember Penelope,

Endymion, and the Lesbian dance.
You look not upon me, but upon
The ashtray and mug of cold coffee

You claim to be accustomed to drinking.
Having shared the cornucopia, the frolics
Of Pan, our friendship must end,

Or Endymion, you fear, will awaken
And flee; Penelope might abandon me,
And your priestesses cease to praise you.

But such is not the gift of Pan,
Is not his nature, nor his intent.
Penelope gives her blessing — she,

Too, lies with Pan, when I am gone.
Endymion, his own eidolon, neither cares
Nor knows aught. Your girls haven't

Danced for you in too many years.
We are *friends:* that we have tread
The circle of Pan does not diminish this!

You did not diminish yourself!
You cannot betray the *idea* of moonflowers.
Beckoning me does not diminish Truth.

So, take my hand, Selena, let us climb
Through your hazel-grove, approach the marble
Stairs to your temple. Pan is all, within.

GATE TO PINEY CREEK

1.

We were given
the moon, the cross,
and a half-carafe
of sparkling water.

2.

We were given
saltfish, wine
for our lips, and
bread for our tongues.

3.

I would give you
my bed, these words,
this wooden gate
to Piney Creek.

4.

I would give you
this spray, my
urgencies — make
of you my current.

5.

If I could
recite the names
of angels, I would
give them to you.

6.

But the names I
invoke are more
earthy — swirling,
milky and primitive.

VERGINE E PUTTANA

Sole fluido – avorio infernale.
Sabbia, il panico
liquido di perpetua alba,
la carne angelica
sulle ossa di bambini nudi.
L'assenza silenziosa
di una neve quasi visibile.

She is yours, yours to penetrate.
Possess the light
Passion, shell and fruit.

GENESIS

It has stopped snowing.
Feast on Eve — labia
and vulva-shell, oyster-
fruit and blood. Gnaw

back to beginnings,
ever back, she the
shellfish poised
beneath flame, she

the nacre, hunger's
source, whence none
who enter ever return.
Set sail, Odysseus!

She is yours, yours
to penetrate. understand.
possess the light of her
possession, shell and fruit.

THE EGG'S RED POOL

COVER US WITH YOUR POOLS OF FIR
(H.D.)

Branches shed their
needles and cones,

concubinal wine
trickles from marble

hands, meteors
sizzle, the colossus

Roars
and on Her knees

it's the wind on the ground, not I, who lifts your skirt to the hips,
the wind who has fingers — mine are numb — and it is Lorca, not I,
who unbuttons your blouse.

I drink your bloody vintage: I extend and forfeit my tongue! I would
be this plummeting valley cradling you and the creek's rampant
libido. Your lap the bed where the unicorn curls, you sink into my
beard. Mine the proud and brimming groin! — mine the breath
igniting your flesh! Ultimate as rain, you permeate —

Beneath absolute black star-bearing silhouettes of silver maple
branches my body churns in yours. Your blood is on the wind. You,
who name yourself *Agony,* whose breasts are
dark upon dark
form from Man's
dark clay
your forests,
fling roots
to writhe restless

in black soil,
lip forth
whole wildernesses!
where the aching stars tremble to fall into your lap, tremulous as I.

like frost over crimson forests or froth of sea-wave over seed-core or
sea-foam's froth over pine-cone, the sea-mare, *Mare,* Our Lady of
Foam, bends sea-mane to flesh to salt-tongue the crimson gold of
pine-grove, foam-sheen over branches; the concubine's crescent her
cauldron caressing scent pine-breath—stroke on spruce their
masculine beards!—inhale their fungus perfumes! A shared breath.
Now it is you whom I am become sea-foam sea-form seed-foam
seed-core sea-maiden sea-mare *Mare Ave Mare* pine-branch curls
over pine-cone fallen salt-soaked fragile gold curl crisp over gold-
flush the black carcass of a jagged pine-trunk.

So ugly I am said
to have beauty,
I awaken to your
gaze from a nearby
log, silking your hair with abalone comb. Behind you, the creek's
foam gathers dawn's plums and apricots; behind me, mists on
mossbeard steam into musk. Your rowan-stained lips ascend my
stirring.

Perhaps I *should*
read Kerouac,
but I'd rather
read you,
seduce you
with cappuccino.

I have spoken,
and I live,
and I kneel

to kiss your loins.

EYE SEA

A sudden flurry
and snow settles

into my eye as
drifts
                expand, each
more
                            infinite...

blown
further and further still
now all I

see
        is snow

drifting
breast-meadow

white —
                calm
now. and settle.

Now rise,
Caw! against
                the
inside

                of my
skull, the outside
of my
eye.

TWO EAST

The ledge.

White lilies snow on white
pond.

ENTER HER TO FIND ME

I peer
            where billowed
       mists disguise
             the deep
ravine I
          see, no
       gaze at,
            no, into,
rather am
          amidst, no,
       am mist
            myself I
know the
          mountain's dark
       ravine as
            tundra flow
or cunt,
          that I
       will go,
            am her
already, but
          will return,
       am here
            turned (I
missed myself)
          here even
       now turn
            not her

PALISADE MESCALITO

ice

chunks
slow Cedar River

earth
bleeds black rocks

dead trees
black cliff

bleeds

ice-leaf river-
leaf

bleeds rock-leaf
dead

tree amulet
charred

carcass

HOME

Pine and virgin snow
mount petrified peaks.

I stumble, not unexpected, near-
blind to the nearest stones. Snow

nymphs chipped by wind
flurry in the lodgepole bearding

alpine faces, emit their brilliant
hiss, pleased to wed stone,

to fall into spring,
the becoming tundra.

My eyes the mirrored
dancers of an ancient dawn,

rise like the lights. Caress me.
Climb me if you dare.

PLACENTA

1.

Sun, from her slow axle,
Reels to the faceted rill—
Shatters in the ruby rill.

I splatter with these
Sharded ripples
My dusty brow.

2.

I stroll naked through this orgy
Of amethyst and lichen—

Constellations; this moraine
A zodiac of boulders.

3.

A flank's hushed ripple—
An elk-stag drifts
Through ruby-barked pine.

4.

We're already *in* the fucking heavens!
Christ!—your perversions!

How dare you judge me!
You virgin! You eunuch!
How dare you presume!

The Horned God squirms,
Turns to be reborn!

5. HIKING

from Silverthorne, Colorado
into Eagle's Nest
Wilderness on the Gore Range
Trail over Red Buffalo
Pass between Buffalo
Mountain and Red
Peak above Willow

Creek's thunderous plummet opiate
falls frothed from June's rich
watermelon glaciers colliding with
that ultraviolet wheel of thaw —

6.

I hear
         — the syrinx?
      — it is faint...
             — that trill!

7.

as from the Oread's
supple moss-
vagina a ruby spring the

cloven-hoofed
God
is kicking

THE PACT

...broach of...lazuli...
...opal moon...reveling...
hair of a pagan...
crown of crows'...beard

...indigo mounts....jaw.
...my brow...constellations
that I...never forget
where...find her...grip

my spirit's maw...
...upon the domes...her
breasts beyond the boundless,
...western sea....she'll gather

my bones, mark my grave
with an unplucked lock...
...-lit pearls, seed-foam,
curl...a nest.

Meditation

sit in a valley
last winter's snow

shrouds the peaks
sit in a valley

gaze at wild rocks
gazing at peaks

watch rocks gaze
I wish I am a mountain

EROSION

a rock pond.
lilies breathe stone.
sun. pond dream.

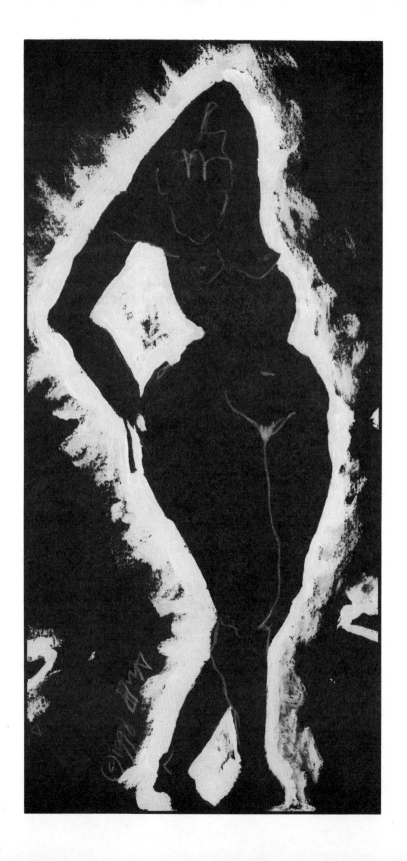

PART 2:

ORGASM

HALLUCINATIONS

ALL ACTS OF LOVE
AND PLEASURE ARE MY RITUALS.
FOR BEHOLD, I HAVE BEEN WITH YOU
FROM THE BEGINNING,
AND I AM THAT WHICH IS ATTAINED
AT THE END OF DESIRE.

(WICCAN CHARGE OF THE
GODDESS, ORIGIN UNKNOWN)

PAN

Your message from that star's
solar plexus means my death. let
the Basarids form a ring, one-
quarter through the night.

> — polar lights, a swan's nape
> and apollo shiva jehovah mithras allah by
> Pan they're the same, all part
> of the Basarids' art.
> Wine, Darling?
> Red Zinger
> to celebrate the Moon?
> the Moon-bearing
> Earth? a toast.
> a wedding is not
> impossible so let the
> ring begin at your side
> sing at your side let
> the ride begin.

I prance for your taste,
I canter around
and round and round.

THE KISS

she drinks — snow
above the jut
of timber pressed
by a rutting sun

Invoking the Moon and Masturbating, Hitchhiking to Cedar Rapids, Iowa from Bozeman, Montana at 3 A.M. on I-90 East, the Road to Damascus

blank
night
milky

sky.

Slow
Silver
Slice —

blood-
meadow.

Split
Head
Bubbles.

stars
careen —
eyes,

Bone,
Torched
Muscle.

APOLLO

(A REPLY TO "ARTEMIS" BY OLGA BROUMAS)

Let's not wage war. A warm palm
smooths the brow along
the ridge
of a troubled thought, invites

any ecstasy once transfixed
on that sheer, sweat-
glazed cliff to return, solid,
to that synchronous first caress.

I comprehend that
spurs —
those lichen-weathered constellations —
mirror the bordering firmament. I am, and I

am man, much more
than a phallic spear. I climb
in gold where timberless peaks
grip the dripping sun

and pull,
securing warmth
against an alpine wind
swirling to

unforming only to re-
appear in forests, the aspen, pine, blue
spruce, the splitting of cones.
What fragrant teeming,
this moment on Earth!

I trust the marbled
geology
of poetics, our own cosmological

rhetoric, yet I am
stunned by the sudden burst
of breast-relentless

snow, from which I must
find shelter
or perish.

PAN

(A REPLY TO "THETIS" BY OLGA BROUMAS)

Arise! The north wind
startles. Wake
among the spruce, come
hearken, come climb.
                              Humming-
birds feed, scarlet iris, see

the eagle hunting food for his nest
swoop behind the aspen. See
the sun
jar the high snow, the snow the sun—
that clash of ancient rams. Son, you can see

how wind and wood
create us—here, on this mountain,
we are virile, dwarfed
by peaks, awed by this lake at
timberline, arching trout, ice-blue sky. Here,

the north wind foams like rapids
out of Canada. To warm you,
Son, a woman will come to caress you,

ask you to forget these
sun-blasted peaks, this
aching for stars. She'll offer coral charms
and a kelp-skirted moon. Here
is how you
persuade her. Come gather

reeds

by the emptying stream; come, canter down, find stems
to bind them, stems of young aspen.
Dance here beside me.
Pipe like the frenzied wind.

GARDENWEB

opal moon-
tongue slides

from flagstone
crumbling
sandstone

to rose quartz lily-
of-the-valley
granite to fossilfern

and raspberry, stream — pine-
branch floating
and beaver-dam

from bluff to blue spruce blue
jay crag

                        golden
          eagle
                sapphire

sky

opal
moon-tongue

slides

Two Gardens with Thaw

Wearing February's hiking
boots, the Cedar Rapids sun
splashes across sidewalks,

crunching
snow in small crouching patches.

Last autumn clatters
in the asphalt gutter.

(late April—
Red Sandstone Mountain—

aspen drip
in the afternoon,

boots crack pine-
cones, needles, twigs, wet bark,

crunch over patches of snow.
We trickle with thaw—

lie in red soil—
streams from every finger)

SYRINX

Pungent mushrooms, spruce —
That whorled spear of turquoise —

Heather-braided wind.

Seized in blood from hoof
To horn, my loamy lips

Unfurl and syrinx-pierce
The falcon-wing on blue —
Force from heather warbling

Kindle my hide! I seize the
Blood-compliant dawn.

Of sun I am wing blue

Wind spruce sweating
Mushroom heather-root!

SIGIL

I carve on aspen-
bark with pronghorn

fork a spiral;

beloved of autumn, I
weave a constellation —

syrinx and serpent
bound by a rose,
a roebuck bounds

through thorn-sweet
blood my own blood

drawn for you. Conjure

the crescent, cast
your crimson circle.

ARTEMIS

I trill the
bright nipples of
the black-breasted
night. Am I
the lapping pup
of that she-
wolf? or the
black nymph's lover?
And you, are
your own breasts
bared in dark
supplication? or do
you emulate, or
are you now,
Herself, the night?
and is it
to me that
you beckon, your
crimson and black
skirt unwound and
now spread beneath
you like poppies
in loam? What
tossing disturbance? Is
it for me
your belly ripens?
I pipe in
your pine pungent
greenwood. Do your
swollen breasts brim,
and is it
to me that
you offer your
stellular milk? By
resin-barked wood,
place a single
star upon each
of my horns.

MIRANDA GATHERS

Miranda gathers magic
spills sibylline
laughter from the kitchen
sink where she scrapes
off into the porcelain black
cheddar and tuna
from the prehistoric frying

pan I kiss her ankles my
fingers canter, drip with

vines, linger whence focus
returns, rose, in foam
Miranda, salt-flushed...

...is mermaid mer-
sibyl maid
marred by thrashing
arrows last
night's sperm
of a cheap Denver
cowboy but armed
with the seed-killing
sponge she returns

to my tongue, for I, too,
know men, have eluded
semen, and returned to milk
the sapphic moon,
my spirit, that moist
and willing girl.

Her vines tighten, bristle;
her hand on my blood-root—
Behold Bast!
The spell is cast!

HYALINE

I am the tower
built of blood
over brambles,

built of sweat, your
suicide threats. I
rub the moon, that

pearl — your riptide
undulates, celebrates
your drowning. You

are meat and oyster-
shell, nacre, delicious
raw. Your flesh

like night blankets my flesh.
You bleed like dawn
where I drift like a flute.

YOUR DREAM, MY VERSION

Sudden with sweat
          and sodden, dazed
     by your tongue's wordless
            urging, I shower you

in semen which rills
          from your bubbling,
     glistening lips,
            mats your ear's

felt down,
          pools in your black
     hair fanning
            across satin

like peacock's plume,
          pools in your pillow's
     warm basin.
            A second shudder

gels into aureoles
          about your nipples,
     wings upon your
            wrists and palms.

A growl, atavistic,
          wells from the caves;
     your moistures break
            and I am hurled

to a sudden curl,
          a crescent's heave,
     your belly sudden
            with sweat and sodden.

PASIPHÆ

The sun, that
mad bull,

hoists on his horns
whole forests.

You, his mount,
recline on wet grass,

open *full out*
your nacreous lips,

and lick from smoked
oysters their oil...

what of you the
sun-god would

scorch remains cool:
your well-turned

tongue oblivious to
the molten, blinding

horns, licks
from oysters their oil.

Your blood a wash
on his sky, the spent

bull snorts whole
clouds; you chortle

and drift — to a shell-
fish moon.

ORGASM HALLUCINATIONS

Barge of gold on honey-
           suckle waves, saffron
       rain, wind-driven
                   nectar, gilded Buddha.

                     π

Your blood the swollen Ganges;
           my sperm the White Nile;
       from tongue to tongue retsina
                   passes; your nipples olives,

your sweat mad honey,
           my testicles mussels,
       my eyes the sibyl's vapor
                   you gasp in, gasping me.

                     π

All darkness cardamom —
           your pelvic lips, satin
       crescent; rare, incessant
                   rowing — cardamom.

Garden of Passion/
Garden of Love

A comet roars
Its white horse
Thorns

The unicorn
Reclines
Into marrow

OXYMORA

Yours the veiled menhir — incontinent ruby,
Erect, the orphic flush in a wasteland

Of mirrors. Your miracles of mirth

A mire of hysteria — you splinter your
Mocking-glass to mutilate

Ghosts and men. Yet you *are*
The obsidian vesicle, erosion's pearl,
Your waxen bowl an antediluvian

Lullaby in Bacchic luster.
Inside the boulder, springs; in woods

Semilunar, holly, wild apples,

And roebuck. In you the emerald
Tablet, emerald egg, and python.

WAXING

O pale daughter
of blood-relentless
memory I thought
I knew the mouth
which spoke me
you beheld me
beneath your
rose-cauldron
incantatory
mouth erect
as a man
could be and
waxing still O
salt of blood
and tears your
taste the galaxy
that binds us

PART 3:

COLD WOMB.

WET WORLD.

THE BLOOD-DIMMED TIDE IS LOOSED,
AND EVERYWHERE THE CEREMONY OF
INNOCENCE IS DROWNED...

(WILLIAM BUTLER YEATS,
IRELAND, 20TH CENTURY)

Moon-Rose

Wrist-blood red,
the rose bursts,
glutting craters
with blood, fire
And thorns.

Blood dancing
Off your arms, you
scrawl your suicide,
agitate the moon's
motionless dust.

Swollen in flame,
You burst into a rose-
Petal sleet—a
Bloody blaze,
Your own last dawn.

No one lives there.
The sun does not look
At all the same.

You press your wrists with thorns,
lament the Moon as dead, and
press each thorn carefully deeper.

FROST

She said, *I'll be your
depth-hoar.*

*I'll be your
surface-hoar, too.*

PAN

a neon scrawl
on your hard
wood floor the
lake of blood
a red hill
side mere smear
in a black
lake's belly you
carved both wrists
with a steak
knife *danced before*
Death, you said,
then laid that
ghost of unholy
dust with the
sacral lust of
a virgin reborn!

The Fury of Snow

Groping through a blizzard, blood
Expands into crystals, flesh drops

In frozen chunks. My heart spits

Trails of pink, slides from my frost-
Bitten crotch, splattering a drift—

Swift cover of wind, and it's buried
Through the winter, so hard it must
Be marble. A single eye remains,

Open. I snap in three: my head
Is in the river. The crotch is food

For wolves. My carcass can't be found.

The eye, groping on the slivered
Moon, is hunter-like, and howling.

blood.
So naked,
then,
she...

THE CONFESSION

The day she jumped and kept falling
you saw her

blood. So naked, then, she
hadn't seen the garden
for so long.

An emerald-skinned serpent
curled, cracked the emerald egg.
Shell-shattered, she was here.

She jumped
and you fell with her.

Like being all white in woods.

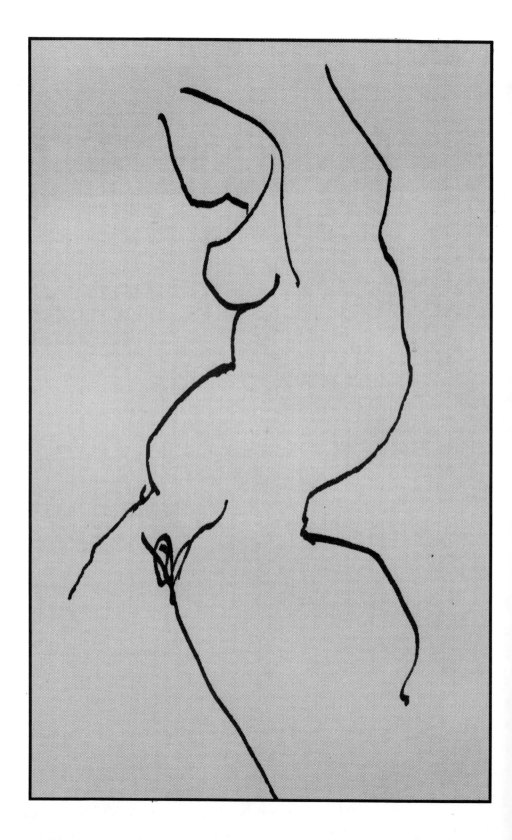

IN PRAISE OF DEATH

STONE, STONE, FERRY ME DOWN THERE
                    (SYLVIA PLATH)

Cold shards crackle
One upon the other —

Brief veils swell in
Circles upon the froth —

O, that dripping mouth

      stone, stone

Philtered with death,
Prayer and perfume.

LETHE'S WHORE

By the steel lake's slim
Tide I watch her swim

To vulviform

Chalice waves. She
Offers herself more.

The waves are cupped hands—
As each one lands she
Feigns like a whore.

She is half-storm.
Her thousand breasts supple

Drift to me on ripples.

She's become the heiress
To foam. Useless.

AN EPITAPH

the black cliff
thunders its share

of thaw

nearby
a lily floats

ANGEL FLESH

Her lacquer-handled glass reveals the rose
Of her ascension; certainly, she'll see

She isn't ugly there. But cast across

Her torso, petals; thorns adorn her warm,
Still-trickling breasts; her bedroom walls — by flung

Blood stained — a Rothko canvas; drifting, strewn
Black hair, solicitous blue gaze, and pale
Serrated blade — in currents of Herself

Adrift. Her dance mænadic, lewd, devout,
And Death relished his banquet. Courtesan

Of fragments, bride of saviors, telepath —

She cast her pulse's fountains. Death — he kissed
Each tide — adored, adored the angel's flesh.

PAIN PENETRATES

ME DROP
BY DROP
           (SAPPHO)

WHEN ONE IS PAIN

There is no pain;
there is, like
snow
in summer
above timberline,
slow decay —
a crust of ice
near numb
to the assassin
sun until
again

all she
sees
is snow.

IMAGE OF THE UNREAL/
IMAGE OF THE REAL

Stoned on coffee at 2 a.m.
Stella in my left hand, a
Lighter in my right.

I was born to the
Human Principal — gradual
Destruction of a planet, an embryo
Soaked in plutonium, how lack of space

Facilitates abortion,
The loss of that silence
Surrounding a stream.

$$\pi$$

I ask for a different home,
A voice from the slivered dome.
Stars have become so important.
Trout, campfire, and tent.

she jumped and kept falling
you saw her.
blood.
So naked,
then.
She . . .
Her impassable crimson lips conceal a

THE CRIMSON

THE FUNCTION OF POETRY IS RELIGIOUS INVOCATION OF THE MUSE; ITS USE IS THE EXPERIENCE
OF MIXED EXALTATION AND HORROR THAT HER PRESENCE EXCITES.
(ROBERT GRAVES)

With icy talon — quivering crescent —
The terpsichorean courtesan

Ascends at bloody dusk; her crimson

Lips, impassable, conceal
A cave of veils; her kiss betrays

A silent well of vestal foam.
A lunar embrace — concubinal arch —
Enflame! her nuptial-cry, mænadic,

Shrill, tumultuous. My mangled
Tongue a scarlet flood in her froth-

Filled chanting, churning mouth.

Her talon — quivering crescent — taut,
Withdraws my dripping, mortal heart.

SONG OF THE DAUGHTER

Your daughter's blood streams
To thighs spiraled by flame.
You curl your curdled lips,
Believe your pillar of blood
Is every daughter's dream.

My horror, spilling blood.
A vestal angel reddens
To black around my womb —
That frozen embryo my Father's
Curse and thunderbolt.

She flies apart: her arm
Bobs from a crow's nest,
Her blood roars into Plathean
Flowers — *stone, stone* —
While Patchen's lion crushes
Her gazelle-throat of dream.

A rising pearl calms
The spinning stars into tender
Focus. The moon-witch
Stills the cunning, the churning
Sea, before angel-flesh
reddens its blackening swell.

SONG OF ULYSSES

I lie upon the banshee-
Currents which render me
Shapeless in a churning
Galaxy, a threnody
Of waves lulling words
Into stars and foam
Into the undressed
Flood of your white skirts.
I am capable of drowning!
I drown a dozen times,
And to still the churning
I become the storm's
Still center, but the trident
Breaks aft as a harbinger
Of rocks I must grasp
Or be broken by their faces,
For you have tossed me here
Among reef and cliff
To run me through
To hollow eyes.
I am capable of loving—
I love once, though to know
The Siren's tongue become
The storm's still rock.
Your charms surround
My lull with a madness
Of spells I must grasp
Or be broken by their mirrors,
For I have felt you here
In this song to your absence—
You haunt me still
And through. Your lips
Pierced—I lie upon a shore
Which holds my briny
Shape in the sands, trembling

By a stream made cold,
Clear by mountains of thaw,
Flooding fingers of white
Foam on your white
Skirts we lie.

THE MIRROR

SHE GRABBED THE ROSE'S STEM.
SHE DIDN'T EXPECT TO BLEED.

In rose-drawn blood
a mirror — *Leuke* comes as
Ulysses strokes and
strokes
the lapping ocean,
strokes the laboring breakers.

Penelope waits, unfurling
to a shell-sharp strand
her shroud of raw silk.

He's washed ashore
when she is naked, weary,
and nearly blind.
A tremble
of flesh more human
than the soul
novas into *Eros* —
lightning splits
the moon — her ocean-
blue eyes into rough silk swirl,

while Neritos fades
to a summit of ice.

COLD WOMB. WET WORLD.

Cold womb. Wet world. A red peak adorns her palm. A sweat of cold mist yet lingers whence God lies strangled in the shadow of polished obsidian cliffs. A mist lingers on that Shore of Bones.

A uterus hovers, a colossus guarding a grey, silent bay. A bronze-phallused man skims the Hyaline, grey fluid sun flecked across his prow. He sees his mother naked, her skin lactescent, grey cloud across her brow. Knowing not-knowing,

> that nimble girl
> > with ankles bare
> once tied the sky

to her waist with a white cord and summoned a phalanx of rainbows to protect her with mica swords and shields of dew from the young men she menaced with her childhood's final laugh and the threat to grow

> > breasts; the moon

catapulted so high that the waking stars fled. Now, she mounts the mist amidst a new tumult of stars, knees and ankles stained by the last blood-anguish of her fertility. She believes no man is near.

$$\pi$$

Wine from God's lips
Still fresh upon her tongue —

> *A man's nipples are*
> > *purposeless, but*
> *for this — I will*
> > *kiss them as though*

74

they were woman's,
> *to instruct. Lie*
with me in Samsara,
> *lie with me and*

sip the spray from your
> *lurid stars' cascade.*

She butchered God, that minotaur, whose seed eddied bubbling to the Styx, whose brain, helplessly warm, drained from His eye-sockets where her bronze-phallused son....

Flesh so different
On psilocybin, his
Blood intact, he
Masturbates to death,

The minotaur's skull his
Love-feast. First, his mother
Trapped the beast, betrayed
His leering tongue —

> *Ascend with salmon,*
> *Great God, ascend!*

Whispered into the
Moon-blanched,
Kaleidoscopic wind.

π

Singeing the edge of his mother's suicide, his semen streaks God's inner skull. *Now, will you open your legs?* he cries.

Haze or angel-wisp,
            take the Hyaline's
      bearded pilgrim once
                  again to your bosom!

She turns.

It is not the
            pounding of genitals,
      nor the sweat it
                  calls forth; it
is not the great
            Fuck which makes us
      holy. It is that the
                  rose of my belly
and the rose of your
            heart are one, that
      reveling in you, I must
                  unravel myself.

Pockets of snow begin to strobe between still-descending stars.

Now, return
            to the womb, Pan,
      for in your hands
                  my flesh is mere song.

Gatto nero sotterato
dalla prima tempesta del mondo!

her suicide a neon scrawl on minotaur-hide the bay of blood a mere
smear in a blacker lake's belly red hillside she carved her wrists
with a steak knife danced before death than laid that ghost of
unholy dust with the sacral lust of a virgin reborn

76

P.S. I Am Now A Tree

I wound up in a
Place.

A
blood-
filled
room

Where life was literal
(guttural) ambiguity

And Two East was a stagnant
Refrain. O,

To rest
Awhile
And leaf.

PREMONITION OF REBIRTH

All is flame that was not flame
Before. Fire bleeds beneath snow.
Light scorches the palm of God.

In penance for the flame He Himself
Brought to ignite the brittle
Human skull, Prometheus came,

Clapping his one hand until it bled
To its human, mortal core. The poet
Bleeds calm in his savior's palm,

Swallowing flame and nail,
Blazing like a Witch
For the travesties of a meaner God.

I NAME MY GOD

I name my god by grain—barley, maize;
By coconut and quince, olive—name

By fruit my god; by moon—crescent, owl;

I name my god by flesh—diamondback
And salmon, pheasant, elk, buffalo.

I eat my god and know *myself* as food:
My ego's blood, fermented, draught of ghosts;
My corpse my gift to maggots, crows, or flame.

I feed my god with sex, masturbate
And couple: burrow, bliss, baste in sweat;

I feed my god with art, muscular;

I feed my god by thaw, thunder, snow.
We salivate, convulse, share one skin.

PART 4: MNEMOSYNE

Because you love the Burning-ground, I have made a Burning-ground of my heart—That you, Dark One, haunter of the Burning- ground, May dance your eternal dance. Nothing else inhabits my heart, O Mother. The funeral pyre blazes day and night, and I have preserved the ashes of the dead, Strewn all about, to welcome your coming. With death-conquering Mahakala beneath your feet, Enter me, and dance your eternal dance, that I may behold you with closed eyes.

(Bengali Hymn to Kali)

ELLIPTICS

Mild anarchy here.
We mumble 'bout
That bony shore

Swiftly passed. Passing Charybdis
Remains, as
Caught by gestures we bob

At gravity's edge.
Incontinent sea, what a ledge to drop
From, thick dust-layer

Atop each ticking wave. Mired heads
Nod, blnk. Perplexed,
Perhaps. *This is not what it used to be, not*

to be, this passage. Monoliths
remain. So do gestures.

1:11 and my pants are down.
No sand on the bottom of this

Ocean. No bottom at all.

Sometimes the Vision
Seems Lasted Out

Keep your right eye closed.
Tilt the paper sideways. Drink two
Pots of Sulawesi, light the stellar gold
And smoke two packs of Camels.

Daniel loved Corinna. Corinna
Loved me. Daniel and I loved Corinna.
Jason loved Rachel, and I loved Rachel's sister.
Jason loved Rebecca and I loved Rachel.
Daniel married Rebecca. Daniel
Loved Jason. Daniel loved Rebecca. Rebecca
Loved Daniel and Jason loved Corinna. Jason
Loved me but I feigned sleep.
Brandon loved, but was never loved
Enough by a woman to love
How he deserved to love.
Virgil loved Steven. Steven loved Virgil.
Virgil loved Cynthia, but Cynthia left with Steven.
I loved Rebecca, and Daniel loved me,
Stroking my rectum, provoking
an anger so perverse
I nearly sacrificed his head to the drywall.
I left Daniel with Rebecca so Daniel still living loved Rebecca
And I stared at the Flat Irons for the next several hours.

I loved Kassandra. I used to love
Kassandra. Kassandra loved me, Ophelia did not. Kassandra loved
Reginald and Miranda loved Virgil.
Kassandra, Ophelia, Miranda and Eve were all one
Kassandra, but they forgot about each other a lot, and I
Haven't seen Kassandra in over a year. I loved
Alice, in interlude, with Virgil,
Because Alice had never had two men before.

P.S. To Miranda

Gandalf is a massive beast, black-
Shining as a panther. Iowa
(the rapists lurking to ambush you
behind the Dairy Mart;
My evenings at the Center for Substance Abuse,
For blotter meditations on sophistry's defense;
And whether I made enough love to you
To forgive your suicide,
Before the neutron bomb or a Palo meltdown;
But poetry on-line with Ari the Fresian?)
Will be left behind—as expected,
I'll be ever averse to
Returning, my gut knots up to a gnarled pine.
I'll spend the summer at home in Colorado,
Beaver-quilted valleys tassled with brooks.
I desire the wisdom found hiking,
Ambling through rivers, gnawing pine needles
And spitting them out, silences surrounding streams
And between winds, myself a mere speck when
The universe below timberline explodes into gold.
I can shiver in the real world,
In darkness alone beneath a lone black fir and stars, where a
Snowbank starves, and grind my own Sumatra beans.
I won't hike down till mid-autumn.
Then into a coven—
My roots
Are in the stars, my temple where I stand.
Showers in a water
Fall dreams of a dryad.
Just so you know
Not to shade me
Here, I'm gonna be a Witch.

Listening

Spring trickles squeak ticks, mosquitoes;
Elk strangle on ranchers' wire;
Hibiscus.

I hike a cleft,
Waking patches of soil
To the careless crunch
Of good boots on sagging snow.

Blue spruce
Branches slap my thighs
As I leap from granodiorite
To silver-plume and
Still higher the peak
Drawn to me
Thawing
Catches my breath
I gnash with bared teeth
First nettles to a low
Branch stoop for rosehips

and I would tear into cracks
like a doll into stuffing
or a cliff into stars but
am too damned pleased
laughing at the sun
which is so *close* here

π

I build me a fire
near the thawing ledge
and sleep easy in my old red bag
listening to the avalanche come

First the slow

Creak of dawn; then, like
The babble of stars
A crack wombs its heavy
Yawn, the cry opens
Its first mouth, that slow
Roar of cliffs. What
Tumbles down are
Children, milking

Snow. I slap my knees,
And cackle like a shaman.

How Leucosia Became
A Blue-Eyed Raven

Rainbow surround moon
Like whirling 'round bonfire.

Thirteen women throng
'round bellowing horny goat-foot god.

My horns don't sparkle
Yet to yer tongues crackle!

> *Ah...aum...and so I embrace*
> *The blest of your race*
> *The beast of your race*
> *The breasts of your race*
> *And so I embrace*
> *The blest breasts of your race*
> *So early in the morning!*

Ah, being! To be! Mænad's god!
Bacchæ-chant and thrum!

Blesséd bare-breasted Basarids swarm
Through thickets of thorns to a pallid,
Drowned, beached-up, *Lethe*-drowned shambles.

Mmm, she was a blue-eyed, corvine-
Haired, coral-lipped, niveous-fleshed
Raven. They flushed her from brambles —

A goddess, *ah...aum...*marble, er, marvel
Aphrodite — the Siren whose philters
Straightened Odysseus's masthead.

Mast-tied Odysseus
A helpless drunk
A saving Witch's lees

> *Ah...aum. And soon they tumbled down.*
> *Deck-chunks, masthead,*
> *Slimy with goat-sperm*
> *(and the head of the guy*
> *who was pierced in the eye)*
> *And they all came,*
> *All came*
> *All came tumbling down.*
> *Then, only Sea, and Ulysses.*

π

A Nereid, Nereid
Flung me her scarf
A Nereid set me ashore
(I couldn't but see that naked was she...
A willing-glance and a Satyr's trance...
I'd promised to toss it back);

From me she received, deceived, my seed,
And you, *O Thálassa*, Great Sea, Great Sea,
O she was received by you, and She,

Received, recedes, recedes;
Great Ocean, Great Sea,
A *tássaná* through whom I

Bubble. flail. swim.
Find wood. and gnaw
Till my claws
And teeth redden, redden, redden your beach.

And on this island, Cycladean gem
I find, not condoms,

But *thyrsus!*

A rainbow surround moon.
Thirteen women throng round bonfire,
Chant to a single drum the threnody —
Dead, Immortal! Mount Her, O Pan!
Stroke with phallus, vanquish Death!

HOLDING TOGETHER

You ask me not to leave then not to stay
Then not to come inside
But I come as the rose that grows through snow
The only rose I know
It was yours and I left for this
Was what you wanted.

I'm not as humiliated as you
Accuse but the smell
Of Old Bushmill's is too strong
When you lift your skirt and point
then call me back forgive my
Leaving you you ask me not to love
Before we love you claim it's not
The seed that's killed by the I.U.D.
But the feminine radiata and I don't mention
That there's really no difference made
I should have spoken then at any rate
You refuse condoms say that tonight

Is the end you call me
To give me what I deserve
Because you deserve it but
Mostly because I love you and we love
Once again. Come, come again?
But now more aloof it's fun and I really believe
It's better like this I didn't know how
Dependent I had become it comes
from me and I prance the goat
Through your room
Your warm and trembled thighs
Muscled tight around my buttocks
Your arms about my shoulders it comes we both
Come twice I know it's true

For you shudder with Pan
Awake all night I love you don't want you
To come alone and tomorrow morning I
Reading Euripides you bleed you say you
Bleed you ask me not to come
To come I come you say you

Are glad that I came
You argue that you might need yourself
But the Ego is not I wonder never the Self
So I leave as you ask you ask me
To come again. Come again? You ask me
To come again. While he who kisses your breasts your

Pride and *Joy?...beautiful lady,* he calls
You you ask him to leave because he
Can't be seduced? Back in Two East I
Come to you once and you weep and I don't
Come again until you call and we
Love until tomorrow I call you tonight
And another man answers but

It's really you

Baritone, with seven shining steak knives
Dangling from your wrists

The Sirens hum the paramedics come
I come running exhausted I come
As the rose that grows through snow I come
As they lead you away but you
Left your purse inside
And the *(I'M SICK I'M...)* blood on *(...A CIRCUS...)*
Floor is *(FREAK)* legible with one shining

Steak knife rippling still lapping the blood from
The well on your bedroom floor whence it springs
To the walls I know
It's because I'm yours you love me but not
Because you told another man you loved me
Which is why he left said he wouldn't
Come again.

You sail through the jagged
Reef I come with visions of my own suicide
(Will you marry me?)
You tell me I had no right to let you live
Like I have no right to love you
(you had an abortion
at age fifteen).

You leave in December
Return in January (come, come
Again?) to claim it's my fault it's I
Who belong in Two East

Then you sit on my lap to *comfort* me

But I cannot eat your walnuts and sprouts Jack cheese
To tell me what I've become.
When I leave I stop
By an exhausted snow and I left my hand to melt.
For seven long seconds.

You call me from Arkansas
When you know I've found Amrita
you called me to say she *deserved* me.
Yes, I say, *she does.* I ask how you
Knew and you

Whisper something about souls,
Something about *our child,* and you ask
Whether I am really this cold or just feigning
And you think I really love *you* but wouldn't (I

Come again?) *admit it.*...There are some days
And nights when I don't even think of you
Now.

DRIFTING APART

I write with wooden
Cock the green word —
I am the cloven hoof.

I am on your cliff
By bloody nails,
My moon — from the ivory
Forest on the slopes
Of yonder mountain
Seeds soar,
Each in wet
Dream. An icy
Wind quaffs
Clover and foam, thistles
Writhe an entire bridge,
A crow commands a dove
Into the serpent's eye.

Scarlet-soaked winds
Siphon blood from a virgin's
Mouth, shed roses
Which yank me like hooks
To the parting of waves,
Your tight caress,
Your cave of bones
And wavering light.

I splash in your magenta,
A blot against rainbows
Rippling black.
I drink your chilling foam.

Your palms fade, cupped,
To scaled thighs —
I churn against the darkness.

I am the goat your own tongue
Craves. I would plow your bloody
Waters, but words unfold from your labia, converge
On your tongue's red mound like luminous fish.
Their flames must not consume me!
Mine are horns of lightning born!

Yet my bones slither
Through skittering eddies;
My heart strolls
Across wave-crests;
My balls bob
And freeze into foam.
I am strewn to a permanent grave.
Your rigid breasts, buoys, consign my last
Fragments to the current.

You use cocks, wear them
Wrapped like charms
Around your wrists.
The moon's maw crunches
The forest. Rivers of blood.
Words collapse.

Drifting apart,
While a galaxy spins
Between us, we
Are spoken.

And we are not,
As per Mr. Lawrence,
Animals driven by ritual
Instinct, but human
Beings driving ourselves
Into a vast Uncertain.

THE FLANNEL SHRED

She hunts at night.
Mine the mountain's
Beard and balls,

She the sentient
Storm strained
From willow's bark,

Her fingers kneading
Sky into asphodels,
Stars curving

Their trauma light
Back to her brow.
She bends to a bed

Of bent currents,
Quick to remark
Awry the dryness

Of webs, sundry
The shadows on her
Shoulders' rise, her

Breasts flecked with
Light when wading.
She hunts. This moon

Her shred of flannel,
Mine the blood
She heaps into

A chair, the swan's
Neck risen
By teeth, chortling

For semen. I shed
My condom like a
Rattler's coil.

She hunts at night.
My bewildered limbs,
Dismembered, float.

WHEN THE RAINBOW NODS OFF

CANTO ONE: BIRTH

I am a body and I
splash in the great red eye
until I land on a life —

seed-foam surges to coral
reef to crescent;
an ocean of flame
stuns the Arctic
egg — scarlet spray
ablaze on that taut moon.

Her strange and sacred shelter,
Caverna d'ossa —
Her gentle haven, Her circle of flames.

Living, I must find Her,
though lizards are born and decay
stoic at my very feet.
I pluck two strings for Charon —
his hollow eyes see
but what they see I can't sing
so I place that piece of gold
beneath his tongue, and board.

His beard
presses soft against my palm.

*The sea
restores....*

I pluck one string to break
the craft's swift silence.

        drop
                        after
                drop on my face
                                white
        water
                        erupts
                mountain
                                mist
        drips
                        needle
                bounces
                                bark

vanishes eyes tongue beard
my head appears
sliding from silk the curl
of Her lips summits surge
azure and warm into trickling,
raspberry, sage, silver ore.

Was it his voice
or Hers? *The sea restores....*

(Her gentle haven, Her circle of flames,
Her strange and sacred shelter)

CANTO TWO: INITIATION

We are one tribe,
the belching and blind,
we grovel in our groans,
the agony of pheromones.

A garden of gods — red
sandstone boulders — rough breasts
on hills of granite streams of pebbles.

Small boy, white shirt,
black plastic glasses,
crew cut
shatters marbles against
one stone breast.

I board Charon's barge
alive

(Eurydike, sleeping, shrieks.)

Wearing hiking boots alone,
I pull close scrub-oak
branches to climb the first cliff.

Colorado streams are mead
from melting snow, beaver-
dams, splay of indigo larkspur,
trout and pine. *Tread softly.*

A lizard mounts my leg
but falls to the pluck of my lyre.

Yes, he smiles, *so you must.*
Play for me.

To savor the scent of pine,
to lie belly-down in the forest of pine,
I laugh, tremble and, soaking,
my rags are far below; green
needles flare from my chest.

Her falcon-face a raging mantra,
A genuine immortal
Spiraling from Her summit

Her naked stare, Her swoop and screech,
Her moon-charged talon-
Rage of hunger.

For what is, "crucial"
is sometimes necessary —
your own black piece
of the ripping maw!

CANTO THREE: LOVE

The lizard sings,
I will need a rope
to reach you a rope
to pull you down;
some of your words
have wings, but
not your balls!

(whispers) *...bt thiz*
Magdlyn n mizlokazion
wl mak ye zalivat,
mak yer blude leap
fer itz grate wite
zpray o wale th moment zhe
wirlz an yer prigg
iz zplatterd wi zuz-kum.
zhe'll evn letcha
zum nzid — all ye gotta
do iz zuk-zuk
til ze brainz kum
tumbln down
an out yer manlee
bellee! Tell her,
he yelps, *I'm a man*
who loves from the inside
out, so transfer
your spin, you dervish,
'round me, and I'll
show you an oyster
in orbit! I never
wanted the evil
eye, nor the salt

behind your left
shoulder. I want
your love, a mossy
retreat, and to
beam my pulse
aboard your aura!

Works every time,
y'know?

The lizard mounts my leg
but falls to the pluck of my lyre.

encaged, enraged Her
cave-foam slides
as blood upon my hands.
Blood-foam lifts to Heaven
Her smeared and dripping smile.

The glacial sky
unfolds its rose,
my veins quiver taut
to Her jasper eyes,
Her mouth's familiar froth,
Her rowan lips, Her warmth,
my pool of white within Her palm,
Her strange and sacred shelter.

I am a body
and I splash in the great red eye
until I land on a life

I transform   flesh
into feast,

thighs of peach
and oyster-hair.

Clouds rage
like love rage, the rage
of flesh the feast
rages on.

     I crawl
               into love on
         Squaw Pass
                    tundra
   timber
             moraines
        ranges vanish
                warmth

and by our
heads blooms
part their seed-
foaming lips.

CANTO FOUR: REPOSE

Emerald in a jagged line, and
Azurite, petrified water.
Circe, white falcon.
A branch, its bride of snow,
thick mandala curls
upon juniper.

I am a twisted
pine to a cliff.
It is hardly serene,
but I need these gnarled
roots, my only brace.

(my rags ashred
so I dance bare-assed
in rapids where pebbles
babble about my thighs
near the hairy cave
named *Sentience)*

Ablaze,
talons taut on cliff.
Clouds darkle,
sprout from snow —

My leathered hide
hallucinates Eurydike,
Persephone, underbrush,
Her circle of flame, my haven.

The scarlet hillside —
astonished to cinders at that leap of white

trickling obsidian
cliffs.

(spray of scarlet rust
on a sharp stone sea)

last thought was *...tender star*
of triple flesh, sleep through rage.
The earth — She bleeds for you.

CANTO FIVE: DEATH

For this final ecstasy, you must but follow Her,
your body impaled for the Harpies to pluck—
what awesome food, your body!

gold curls, salt,
deep reds spill,
white lilies snow on white
pond.

Marble dunes.
Ants breed
Marble cracks,
Lizards' shade.
Crumbled marble
Flanks. Cacti-
Sharp patches
Root on Her
Marble breasts.
(snapping fingers.)
Eurydike's blood

will tell

in this
marble cave,
secret cage,
how marble
wills erode—

I am a body
And I splash in the great red eye
Until I land on a life

I transform   *flesh*
into feast

Shrill whispers of shades
garbled through murk

When the rainbow nods off
and the cloud is Ulysses

Steaming with gore!

Coins for the eyes
of that muddied lizard,
Jesus Christ—slush
claws at His frozen face,
Stygian thorns violate
His inopiate palms—
He on His own
infernal stake
is set to flame. A black
diamond for His crackling flesh.

The goat-hooved star-gods dance!

       They shrieked with terror,
       for his loins and belly

       steamed
       and thick

       black blood dripped
       down from both

       *his murderous palms.**

---

[*] quoted from Kimon Friar's translation of *The Odyssey: A Modern Sequel* by Nikos Kazantzakis. The line arrangement is Thornlyre's own.

cold peaks
             stun memory
        flood human
                summit of
    naked forests
          climax
      of flame
              fill
valleys with the roar that outrage
sways
solidity.

Lizards glow
in apathetic preoccupation
where my sandaled feet crunch
what I know are human bones
softened by the slow slide
of lilies and mud.

I seek my helmsman
but I cannot see.

Splashless stream
from obsidian cliff

to pond.
pallid

lilies
float on snow.

The gods swear by this, the mortal
Hollow eyes and ancient beard
Of Charon, his slow rowing...

A man strangles
on the acid sand
of a dying river.

Then the weeds with the tempting
Violet. The Colossus roars, and on Her
Knees,

(abysmal dew—

frozen

crimson void.)

How may I ask
Her to love me?

His beard
Presses soft against my palm.

Her circle of flame,
Her gentle haven.

Mountains blaze from Her hand,
Star meadows bloom into showers
Of lotus-
Fire, eyes too deep to gaze into...

...and I remember what She told
me crawling in,

The sea restores.

The Silver Unicorn

have known the antlered head of my god,
The stars before they were suns;
recall the Moon before She was dust.

BALM

YOUR HAIR IS NOT LESS BLACK
NOR LESS FRAGRANT
NOR IN YOUR EYES IS LESS LIGHT

(H.D.)

I swagger immured
Upon tundra roseate
With the flicker of thaw.

The wind a balm —
   Ophelia, your hair! —
  Nestles moss-soft
    In my trickling palms' bed.

I remember your breasts,
Wine. We plucked
Chorees for our press
Whose juice, as we lay,
Surged about our lips.

I stride bare-soled
    To a glacier, whose melt
  Feeds shelter to trout,
    And plant your breath.

Such roots you spawn!
Whose dragon-weave cracks
The mute permafrost!

Such blossoms you spawn!
   Whose thorned, arterial
  Branches ensnare me — I stagger
    Breast-down to the damp.

remember the Ozarks
y thumb — the baby blue back
f an old Ford truck
/here honeysuckle spun
runkenness into your hair.

/ith what umbilical flood
          Are you fed? Has the cataract
      Broken beneath us?
                Ear to the tundra —

es, a waterfall plunges.
i *amo* ascends.
he spawning of trout.

PLANT ON MY GRAVE
A LOCK OF YOUR HAIR

The speckled breath
Of a nippled sun, a
Fish without a fish,
A lemon-drunk cobra
With wings of bone
Caves suspended
Over bone oceans
And frozen crimson
Eyes; the charred
Wind, its fragment-
Tossed curls
Clotted with bone
Birds, sweats
Its crimson sleet.
Far into the tumble,
Do not think this
Too hilarious: at the
Hull of this mystic
Spoon with shoulders
Spinning loose, slide
Into the grin
To be spat out again.
Nipples of bone wind-
Chimes thrashed
By bone currents.

HAVING HEARD PAN

The windsplitting
spruce the glasschitter
snow my chattering

saw. My worn
boots crunch their trudge
through pathless,

Drifting aspen.

Colophon: God & Unicorn

Reduced to slavering intelligence,
Your virile God—that feral rapist—licked

His fingers raw of you, and reminisced,

Exulting in the blood you shed for Him,
That darkness you once blazed for Him through snow

Of shattered porcelain, irises in
Shard and sliver blinking, long-lashed, at Him,
His seminalia poised, granting blindness,

You hoped, but not the Son He left in you,
The Son you'd later sacrifice, unborn.

The unicorn upon your lap was I—

I grazed your pearls as if to drink of them,
But I could not your wrists nor womb unbleed.

GLOSSARY

phrodite: goddess of erotic love, rn from the mingling of the severed sticles of Ouranos (*see* Eros) with the a's foam on the shores of Kypris yprus). Aphrodite is often referred by that island's name.

pollo: a mouse or wolf god later entified with music, prophecy and, ally, the sun. Considered in classical xts the son of Zeus and twin brother Artemis (cf.).

rtemis: later identified as Apollo's f.) twin sister; originally the Cave ar goddess of prehistoric Europe d Asia. She survived into classical nes as the goddess of virginity, rests and wild creatures, and the moon.

alanta: heroine whose athletic prowess alified her as the only woman to ard Jason's Argo.

cchæ: also known as Mænads or sarids, devotees of Dionysos, god of stasy.

cchus: also known as Dionysos (*see* cchæ).

sarids: *see* Bacchæ.

st: Egyptian cat goddess.

aaron: he whose eternal role is to liver the souls of the dead to the posite shore of the river Styx (cf.).

rce: falcon-goddess, goddess of rcery, sister of Hekate (goddess of itchcraft) and aunt of Medea. She

figures prominently in Homer's *Odyssey* and Apollonius of Rhodes' *Argonautica*.

Cyclades: the "necklace" of islands directly south of the Greek peninsula.

Dryad: a forest-nymph.

Endymion: so favored by the gods for his beauty that they granted him a wish of his own choosing, Endymion asked for eternal youth and beauty. The gods granted his wish, but cursed him with eternal sleep. The moon-goddess, Selena (cf.) or *Selene*, enamored of this "Sleeping Beauty", leaves the sky once per month to visit him erotically; in this way, she became pregant with the Nereids (cf.), or ocean-nymphs.

Eros: along with Ouranos (Heaven) and Gaia (Earth), one of the triplet children of the eldest goddess, Chaos. Ego-shattering Eros represents erotic love at its most primal and spiritual..

Eurydike: bride-to-be of the poet Orpheus, was struck by a viper as she approached her wedding altar and immediately died. Grieving, Orpheus entered Hades, the land of the Dead, in his fabled, but failed, rescue mission.

Gandalf: Padma Thornlyre's old cat, named for the benevolent wizard in J.R.R. Tolkein's epic fantasies, *The Hobbit* and *The Lord of the Rings*.

Ganges: the holy "mother" river of the Hindus, bathing in which is believed to cleanse negative karma.

Harpies: cannibalistic creatures who are part bird and part woman.

Horned God: after the Bear Goddess, who survives as Artemis (cf.), the oldest deity known to have been worshipped in prehistoric Europe. He is mostly known in modern times as Pan or Kernunnos. The Horned God remains a central figure in Wicca, the thriving pagan religion which survived the Christian purges.

Hyaline: a glassy, rippleless body of water.

Ithaka: the island home of Odysseus (cf.).

Kalypso: nymph of the island, Ogygia, who kept Odysseus (cf.) her captive love-slave for seven years.

Kassandra: Trojan princess, priestess and prophetess considered insane by her fellow Trojans. Having agreed to become Apollo's (cf.) lover in exchange for the power of prophecy, she refused him when he appeared to her sexually as a wolf; Apollo cursed her by ensuring that her prophecies, always accurate, would never be believed. Enslaved by Agamemnon after the Greek victory in the Trojan War, she was murdered with an axe by Agamemnon's wife, Klytæmnestra, and Klytæmnestra's lover (Agamemnon's cousin), Ægisthus.

Latmos: the mountain sheltering Endymion's (cf.) grotto.

Lawrence: i.e., British poet and novelist, David Herbert Lawrence.

Lesbos: island home of the celebrated Lesbian poet, Sappho. It was on Lesbos that the flotsam-head of Orpheus (*see* Eurydike), severed and tossed into the sea by the Mænads (*see* Bacchæ) with whom he had spent his post-Hadean years, finally washed ashore.

Lethe: a river or lake in Hades, land housing the dead, which waters, when drunk, induce eternal forgetfulness.

Leuke: Gk. for "milk"; the American poet H.D. describes Leuke as the island in Hades reserved for Helen, daughter of God.

Lorca: i.e., the 20th century Spanish poet, Federico Garcia Lorca.

Mænad: *see* Bacchæ.

Minotaur: endowed with the body of a powerful man and the head of a carnivorous bull; his image inspired the long-running surrealist journal of the same name, and was a frequent subject of Picasso's art. The Minotaur was finally slain by the Athenian prince, Theseus, with help from Ariadne, a Cretan princess who ultimately wedded Dionysos (cf.) after Theseus abandoned her. *Also see* Pasiphæ.

Miranda: Daughter of Shakespeare's Prospero in *The Tempest*, beloved by the sea-monster, Caliban.

Nausikäa: in Homer's *Odyssey*, the alluring princess of Phaiakia whose attraction to Odysseus ensured his safety in her parents' palace. Odysseus wisely shunned her romantic attachment but, in gratitude, promised her the hand of his son, Telemakhos.

Nereid: *see* Endymion and Selena.

Neritos: the mountain-summit on the island of Ithaka (cf.)

Odysseus: hero of Homer's *Odyssey*; also figures prominently in the same poet's *Iliad*, in several tragedies, and in Dante's *Inferno*, among other works; his story inspired two of the 20th century's literary masterpieces: James Joyce's *Ulysses* and Nikos Kazantzakis's *The Odyssey: A Modern Sequel*.

Ophelia: In Shakespeare's *Hamlet*, the prince's mad sister who committed suicide.

Old Bushmill's: an Irish whiskey.

Oread: a mountain-nymph.

Pan: *see* Horned God.

Pasiphæ: an Amazon woman, mother of Phædra, whose sexual attraction to a bull resulted in the birth of the Minotaur (cf).

Penelope: Odysseus's wife, Telemakhos's mother, and cousin of Helen of Troy and Helen's sister, Klytæmnestra (cf).

Persephone: Goddess of death and rebirth, whose consort is Hades, and in whose honor the Eleusinian mysteries were celebrated.

Prometheus: Subject of Aeschylus's *Prometheus Bound,* a Titan whose gift to humanity of fire was punished by the gods: Prometheus was nailed (crucified) to a rock; his bowels became the daily feast of, variously, vultures or eagles. Along with Herakles, a pre-Christian savior-figure in Pagan Greece. The Romantic poet Percey Bysshe Shelley wrote a *Prometheus Unbound.*

Samsara: a Buddhist term referring to the dualistic illusion which creates our state of suffering; to be contrasted with Nirvana, the bliss of non-duality.

Sappho: the poet of Lesbos (cf.) and priestess of Aphrodite (cf.), considered by many (with Homer the reasonable exception) the world's most notable poet. Plato referred to Sappho as "the tenth Muse".

Satyr: half-goat and half-human in appearance, Satyrs are especially known for their prodigious phalloi and their sexual fondness for any willing partner, regardless of gender or species.

Selena: moon goddess remembered for her attraction to the sleeping Endymion (cf.) and her subsequent bearing of the Nereids (cf.), nymphs of the sea.

Shiva: androgynous Hindu god from whose navel a lotus grows during his sleep. The lotus, Shiva's dream, is the physical universe in which we live, believed to vanish utterly upon Shiva's awakening.

Sibyl: originally the priestess/prophetess of the serpent-goddess, Python, and later of Apollo (who assumed, in patriarchal times, Python's role). Consuming an hallucinogenic honey and breathing hallucinogenic fumes from a tripod, the Sibyl would recite her cryptic, though notably accurate, prophesies.

Sirens: in Homer's *Odyssey* and Apollonius of Rhodes' *Argonautica*, goddesses half-woman and half-bird whose song enchanted sailors to their demise on the rocky shores of their isle, where they subsequently supped upon the warm corpses. Sirens are to be distinguished from the cannabalistic Harpies (cf.), also half-woman and half-bird, who possessed no gift of song.

Styx: the river separating the living from the dead.

Syrinx: daughter of a river-god, Syrinx was amorously pursued by Pan (cf.). She prayed to her father to protect her virginity, and was metamorphosed into a single reed in a vast bed of reeds. Pan, perplexed, sighed and music arose from the reeds. Binding together several reeds of different lengths, Pan named his instrument the "syrinx" after his beloved. The syrinx is more commonly known today as "panpipes".

Tássaná: Thai for "a vision".

Thálassa: Gk. for "sea".

Thyrsus: the wand, often a pine branch, wound with ivy and dipped in "mad honey", said to impart to the Bacchæ (cf.) extraordinary magical abilities.

Ulysses: *see* Odysseus.

POETRY BY PADMA JARED THORNLYRE

PUBLISHED

FIRE QUEEN (& RELATED POEMS: 1986-1989)
MY GURU, MY MIDWIFE (POEMS 1981-1994)
ANGEL FLESH (POEMS 1978-1998)

IN-PROGRESS

BURNING

EATING TOTEM

EROS LIGHTNING/FOUDRE D'EROS
(ENGLISH/FRENCH, WITH TRANSLATIONS BY HÈLÈNE D. BRAUN)

A LIST OF WHAT WE'VE BROKEN

METEOR

WILLOW, HAMADRYAD

AFTERWORD:

SPELL OF PARTING

Galimradel-Ledarmilag — I slice
With golden scythe the mistletoe and vine.

I burn with burrs your photograph.

O Hekate of cinders, blow
This smoke and ash across the snow!

Across this drift-choked, frozen plain,
Away, coy angel, dissipate!
Away from me be ever bound!

O Hekate of cinders, blow
This smoke and ash across the snow!

I turn my back forever now,

And chant: "Io Mafu Velho, Amhest Nu!
Io Hekaté, Kalí, Io Évohé!"